TECHNOLOGY IN
ANCIENT GREECE

CHARLIE SAMUELS

Gareth Stevens
Publishing

Please visit our website, www.garethstevens.com. For a free color catalog of all our high-quality books, call toll-free 1-800-542-2595 or fax 1-877-542-2596.

Library of Congress Cataloging-in-Publication Data

Samuels, Charlie.
Technology in ancient Greece / by Charlie Samuels.
    p. cm. — (Technology in the ancient world)
Includes index.
ISBN 978-1-4339-9633-7 (pbk.)
ISBN 978-1-4339-9634-4 (6-pack)
ISBN 978-1-4339-9632-0 (library binding)
1. Technology—Greece—History—Juvenile literature. 2. Greece—Civilization—To 146 B.C.—Juvenile literature. I. Samuels, Charlie, 1961-. II. Title.
T16.S25 2014
938—dc23

Published in 2014 by
Gareth Stevens Publishing
111 East 14th Street, Suite 349
New York, NY 10003

For Brown Bear Books Ltd:
Editorial Director: Lindsey Lowe
Managing Editor: Tim Cooke
Children's Publisher: Anne O'Daly
Art Director: Jeni Child
Designer: Lynne Lennon
Picture Manager: Sophie Mortimer

Picture Credits
Front Cover: Shutterstock

Alamy: Ancient Art & Architecture 42; **Corbis:** Bettmann 35; **Public Domain:** Marie-Lan Nguyen 43; **Shutterstock:** 1, 13, 24, 25, George W. Bailey 27, Anton Balash 14, Panos Karos 17, Luis Santos 38, Alexander A. Trofimov 6; **Thinkstock:** istockphoto 5, 7, 23, 36, 37, Photos.com 20, 22, 32, 33.

All artworks © Brown Bear Books Ltd

Brown Bear Books has made every attempt to contact the copyright holders. If you have any information please contact smortimer@windmillbooks.co.uk

Manufactured in the United States of America

CPSIA compliance information: Batch #CS13GS. For further information contact Gareth Stevens, New York, New York at 1-800-542-2595.

CONTENTS

INTRODUCTION

The ancient Greeks lived around the Aegean Sea from about 1600 B.C.E. until about 100 B.C.E., when their territory was absorbed into the Roman Empire. They were some of the most adventurous, creative, and ingenious people who ever lived. On the Greek mainland, on the many islands, on the coast of what is now Turkey, and in Greek colonies throughout the Mediterranean, ancient Greeks were

The remarkable buildings of the Acropolis ("high city") in Athens were some of the architectural wonders of the ancient world.

A developed writing system allowed the Greeks to record the results of their studies, particularly of philosophy and math.

perhaps some of the most inquisitive thinkers in history. While technology often improved in relatively small steps, Greek scientists tried to understand why things happened. They enjoyed learning as an intellectual challenge.

WARRING STATES

Ancient Greece was not united. It was a series of city-states, which often fought, but which all shared similar culture and worshipped the same gods. The two most powerful city-states were Athens and Sparta. They were often at war, but sometimes made alliances to fight when threatened by others, such as Persia. This book will introduce you to the most important examples of the technology behind this remarkable period of intellectual development.

TECHNOLOGICAL BACKGROUND

The ancient Greeks emerged in a region that had been influenced by a number of earlier civilizations. The Greeks adopted the achievements of these other cultures. The ancient Egyptians had invented papyrus, which the Greeks used to write on. The Phoenician alphabet was the basis of Greek writing. The Greeks took the coinage invented in Lydia, in

The Greek alphabet was based on Phoenician writing, to which the Greeks added vowels.

modern-day Turkey, and improved it. They built magnificent temples and public buildings from marble, but their private homes were made from the same mud bricks as used by other cultures in the region. The Greeks used plumbing and understood the importance of clean water for health.

LOVE OF LEARNING

Unlike other peoples, however, the Greeks also enjoyed learning for its own sake. They created the first public library at Alexandria to share knowledge. Their idea of carefully observing the world was the foundation of modern medicine and astronomy. Their ways of thinking about the world's mysteries were the basis of modern philosophy.

The Minoans of Crete in the Greek Bronze Age had a complex system of plumbing to provide water for bathing.

AGRICULTURE

Farming was the basis of the ancient Greek economy. Eighty percent of the population worked on the land. Farming was hard work. The soil was poor and the land was often hilly. The staple foods of the ancient Greeks were figs, grapes, and olives. Such crops all needed plenty of sun but not much water.

A farmer uses oxen to plow a field while, in the background, workers harvest olives next to rows of vines for growing grapes.

Olive trees grew easily in Greece, despite the poor soil, mountainous landscape, and dry climate.

Greek farmers plowed their fields twice a year: in spring and in the fall. Their plows were made from wood, and were sometimes tipped with iron. Farmers built terraces on the side of hills to increase the amount of land they could plant. They used irrigation and crop rotation to improve the poor soil.

FOOD SUPPLIES

Barley was the most important crop. It was grown between the rows of olive trees. Fishing was also an important part of the diet. Fish were caught on lines using bronze fishhooks. Wealthy people hunted wild deer, boar, and hare using bows and arrows, nets, and traps.

TECHNICAL SPECS

- Olives were harvested by beating the olive tree with whip-like branches until the fruit dropped to the ground.
- Olive oil was used for cooking and eating, but also as a fuel for lamps and as a kind of soap.
- The Greeks made wine by stomping on grapes. The wine was so thick it had to be strained using a bronze strainer. It was usually diluted with water.
- Raisins were made by letting grapes dry in the sun.
- Farmers kept goats to use for milk and cheese as well as wool.
- Greece exported wine and olive oil. By producing a surplus, the ancient Greeks were able to become a powerful trading nation.

BUILDING

House at Olynthos

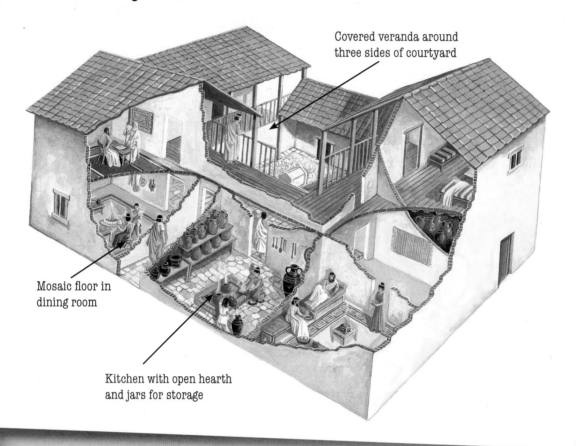

Covered veranda around three sides of courtyard

Mosaic floor in dining room

Kitchen with open hearth and jars for storage

There was a great difference between ancient Greek homes and public buildings. Little remains of domestic architecture, because houses were generally made from sun-dried mud bricks. Temples and the magnificent buildings of the cities were made of marble. Many survive reasonably intact today.

The earliest type of ancient Greek house dates from around 1800 B.C.E. It had a main room or hall, called a megaron, with a hearth and columns to support the roof. From the fifth century B.C.E., houses were built around an open courtyard designed to keep the house cool in the hot summers. There was also a covered veranda along three sides of the courtyard to give shade.

FLOOR COVERINGS

Floors were finished with mosaic tiles in richer homes. In more modest homes, the bare earth was probably plastered or left completely undecorated.

TECHNICAL SPECS

- Wood was only used for doors, window shutters, and roofs, because there was a shortage of suitable trees for building.
- The Greek city of Olynthos was destroyed on the orders of Philip of Macedonia in 348 B.C.E. Its ruins revealed the remains of ancient Greek homes.
- Houses in Olynthos were built in rows on a grid system.
- Women were kept out of view. Their quarters were as far as possible from doors or windows that opened onto the street.
- Bricks for building houses were shaped from mud and left in the sun to dry.

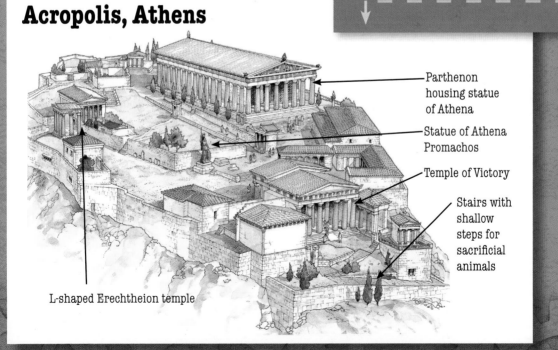

Acropolis, Athens

Parthenon housing statue of Athena

Statue of Athena Promachos

Temple of Victory

Stairs with shallow steps for sacrificial animals

L-shaped Erechtheion temple

PARTHENON AND TEMPLES

Ancient Greek architecture reached its peak in its temples. In Athens, the most magnificent buildings stood on the Acropolis, a rocky hill overlooking the city. The most important building was the Parthenon built for the goddess Athena. Its marble columns made it a template for public buildings.

The Parthenon

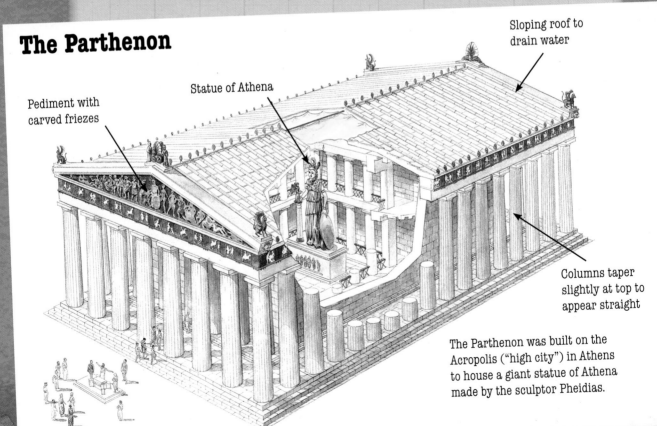

Sloping roof to drain water

Statue of Athena

Pediment with carved friezes

Columns taper slightly at top to appear straight

The Parthenon was built on the Acropolis ("high city") in Athens to house a giant statue of Athena made by the sculptor Pheidias.

Columns were used to create porches outside Greek temples. There were three styles of columns: Doric, Ionic, and Corinthian.

Marble was plentiful in Greece. It was quarried by masons who hammered wooden wedges into cracks in the rock, and then soaked them with water. As the wet wood expanded, the marble cracked. The blocks were shaped in the quarry but were finely carved at the building site. They fit together so well that no mortar was needed.

MAKING COLUMNS

Greek architecture is famous for its columns. Columns were made from squat, round cylinders of marble. To make a column, a number of these cylinders were pinned together using metal clips. The column was raised into place using ropes and pulleys.

TECHNICAL SPECS

- The Greeks used a form of skylight. They placed tiles of very thin marble in roofs to let light through.
- Doric columns were plain at the capital (top); Ionic columns had rams-horn curls; Corinthian columns were decorated with carvings of acanthus leaves.
- The ancient Greeks used an optical illusion in the columns at the Parthenon. From a distance, straight columns look as though they bend outward. To compensate for this, the Greeks made them taper slightly toward the top so that they appeared straight.
- Rainwater drained off temple roofs through spouts carved in the shape of animal heads.
- Decorative friezes were often added to the fronts of temples.

SCULPTURE

This marble statue of the god Apollo was carved early in the second century C.E. It was a copy of a much earlier statue.

Sculptures were used in ancient Greece to decorate temples and other public buildings. They were made out of limestone, marble, or bronze. Sculpture could be statues or friezes carved into the walls of buildings. There were three main subjects for the sculptures: battles, mythology, and Greek rulers.

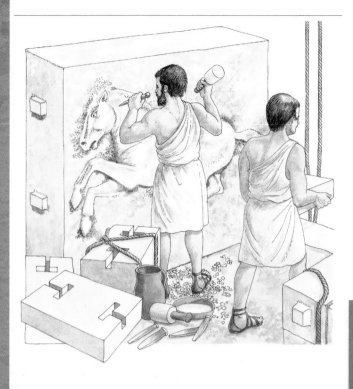

The sculptor first created a full-size model from clay. The marble was chiseled into a rough form by copying the clay model before a master sculptor finished the carving. The surface was smoothed before the marble was painted.

BRONZE STATUES

Bronze statues were cast using the lost-wax method. A wax model was covered with clay, which was then baked. The wax melted and was poured out of the mold, which was filled with molten metal and left to harden. The clay was broken off to reveal the bronze statue.

TECHNICAL SPECS

- Friezes were long, narrow bands of relief carvings that decorated the upper walls of Greek temples.
- Friezes, such as the one on the Parthenon in Athens, were painted with bright colors.
- Statues were finished with metal attachments, such as spears, swords, bridles, and other attachments such as women's jewelry.
- Bronze statues were finished using glass for eyes, copper for lips, and silver for teeth and fingernails.
- Humans and gods were carved at the same size. Male statues were usually young and were often carved nude, in order to show the Greek idea of the perfect human form.

THEATERS

Drama was one of the ancient Greeks' greatest innovations. The word "drama" meant action on stage. Almost every Greek city had a theater that put on dramas as part of religious festivals. The dramas were either tragedies or comedies. In Athens, dramas in honor of Dionysus, the god of wine, resembled modern plays.

The circular space in a Greek theater was known as the orchestra. The chorus performed dances there.

Masks were used to impress or frighten the audience. They also meant performers could play different characters.

Theaters were built on hillsides. They were shaped like horseshoes, with steps cut into the hillside to provide seating. The flat area at the bottom was called the orchestra. It held the circular stage.

ACOUSTIC ENGINEERING

A theater could seat up to 18,000 people, and the people in back had to be able to hear the actors as well as the people in the front row. The Greeks used math to work out the best acoustics. In the theater at Epidaurus, which is still used today, speech from the stage is amplified by the bowl-like effect of the hillside.

TECHNICAL SPECS

- Actors entered the orchestra via a tall arched entrance called a parodoi or eisodoi.
- The seats in the front rows were wooden, so they could be removed; the rest were stone. The best seats at the front were reserved for officials, visitors, and competition judges.
- Stone tokens were used as tickets. They were marked with seat numbers.
- Special effects included a crane (mechane) that made it look as though the actor was flying and trapdoors in the floor used to bring actors onto the stage.
- From 465 B.C.E., a scenic wall was hung or stood behind the orchestra. Death scenes always took place behind this skene (from which the modern word "scene" comes).

SCIENCE AND KNOWLEDGE

The *School of Athens*, painted by Raphael in 1510, shows famous Greek philosophers, with Plato and Aristotle in the center.

The ancient Greeks were the first people to separate philosophy—the study of ideas—from science. Around the sixth century B.C.E., the Greeks began carefully observing the world. This taught them, for example, that sickness is often caused by bad hygiene, not by the gods as had been thought. Observations made the Greeks rethink how they looked at the world.

Although the Greeks attempted to understand more about the world, they did not write down many of their discoveries. As a result, historians once believed that the ancient Greeks had not been interested in science.

GREEK INVENTIONS

Today we know this belief was wrong. For example, the Greeks developed the world's first computer. The so-called Antikythera mechanism was probably used to calculate the movements of the sun and moon. Other Greek inventions included the steam engine and the slot machine. The Greeks loved knowledge. They opened the first public library in Egypt in the third century B.C.E. It was part of the Museum of Alexandria, which was an early kind of research institute.

TECHNICAL SPECS

- The Antikythera mechanism was found in 1900 in an ancient shipwreck. It took scientists a century to realize that it was a computer made up of a series of different-sized wheels.
- Heron of Alexandria invented the world's first slot machine. It was used at temples to dispense holy water for washing as a person entered the temple.
- Heron also invented the first simple steam engine. A pot filled with water was placed over a fire. Two tubes carried steam into a hollow metal ball, where it flowed out through two more angled tubes. That made the ball rotate.

This steam engine was invented by Heron. Steam expelled from the bent tubes made the ball rotate.

ARCHIMEDES

One of the greatest mathematicians who ever lived, Archimedes was also a prolific inventor. Some of his inventions are still in use today. Schoolchildren use one of Archimedes' inventions daily without realizing it: he calculated the value of pi in order to work out the area of a circle.

One of the weapons built by Archimedes to defend Syracuse was a lens that focused the sun's rays to set fire to enemy ships.

HOW TO...

The Archimedes screw pump was a spiral screw inside a cylinder. As the screw was turned, it raised the water from one level to another by pushing it against the side of the cylinder. The ancient Egyptians used the screw to raise water from the Nile to irrigate crops. The screw is still used in many parts of the world today.

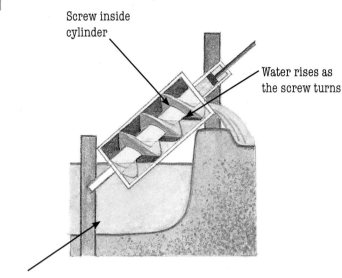

Screw inside cylinder

Water rises as the screw turns

Supply of water

Archimedes was not the first person to use levers, but he was the first person to understand the principle behind them. He calculated the length of lever needed to move any object. He used a lever to single-handedly lift a ship out of a dry dock and into the sea.

WEAPONS TECHNOLOGY

Archimedes invented weapons to protect his city of Syracuse from a Roman attack. He redesigned the city walls to accommodate cranes that dropped large boulders onto the enemy. Another weapon, the "claw," lifted enemy ships out of the water and overturned them.

TECHNICAL SPECS

- Archimedes claw was probably a crane with a grappling hook.
- Archimedes is said to have invented the first fire engine, a cart that carried water.
- Archimedes discovered the principle of the displacement of water when he got into a full bath and it overflowed.
- King Hiero was worried that his gold crown had been mixed with cheaper silver. Silver weighs less than gold. Archimedes measured the water displaced by the crown against the water displaced by a solid gold object of the same weight. He was able to prove that the king had been duped.

ARISTOTLE

Deliquiũ Solis poſt natũ Chriſtum Anno 15 44 die 24 Ianuarij

This 17th-century diagram shows the principle of Aristotle's camera obscura, which projected an image onto a wall.

Aristotle was probably the most influential thinker who has ever lived. His work covered every subject of study known in ancient Greece, including politics, logic, meteorology, physics, and theology. He still influences modern thought. The camera obscura he invented is still used today.

Aristotle tried to separate philosophy from science. He was the first person to spell out that science is based on careful observation. Aristotle proved that Earth is round by observing the curved shadow it cast on the moon during a lunar eclipse.

DEFINING SCIENCE

Aristotle estimated the diameter of Earth to within 50 percent of its true value. He observed that, as he traveled north or south, new stars appeared on one horizon while others fell below the other horizon. This happened after even a short distance, showing that Earth was not very big.

Aristotle was a founder of Western philosophy. He studied with Plato and tutored the young Alexander the Great.

TECHNICAL SPECS

- Aristotle believed that matter was composed of four elements: earth, air, water, and fire. The heavens were made of a fifth, "aether."
- Aristotle believed that the heavens were unchanging and perfect, while Earth was changeable.
- Aristotle's careful observation set the standard for future scientific study. He was one of the first to collect plant specimens and classify them into groups.
- The camera obscura was the forerunner of the modern camera. It was a lightproof box with a small hole in one side. Light from the hole formed an inverted image on the opposite side. The device allowed eclipses to be observed safely.

PYTHAGORAS

Pythagoras was a Greek mathematician, astronomer, and philosopher. He is most famous for the Pythagorean theorem, which is still used in classrooms to help calculate areas.

Pythagoras had many followers. They settled in a Greek colony in southern Italy. Pythagoras greatly influenced the younger Greek philosopher, Plato. In turn, Plato influenced generations of later philosophers.

In this medieval drawing, Pythagoras tests the sounds produced by different sizes of bell and glasses containing different amounts of liquid.

Pythagoras's followers were known as the Pythagoreans. They believed that Earth was a sphere at the center of a spherical universe. They believed that the planets occupied their own transparent spheres. These spheres were spaced out evenly and rotated around Earth.

MATH IN EVERYTHING

Pythagoras believed the whole world could be seen through math. He particularly saw a close link between music and math. He discovered that the intervals between musical notes could be expressed in mathematical terms. Apart from his theorem, Pythagoras's main contribution to science was the realization that answers to scientific problems usually led to new problems.

Pythagoras's theorem says that the area of the square of the longest side of a triangle equals the squares of the two other sides.

TECHNICAL SPECS

- Pythagoras's theorem is about the shape and area of right-angled triangles. The theory had been known to the Sumerians and to the ancient Chinese, but the Greek thinker proved it was right.
- Pythagoras described square numbers, cubic numbers, and spherical numbers before they were fully understood.
- The Pythagoreans treated men and women equally, which was unknown in ancient Greece.
- Pythagoras left no original writings, so everything we know about him comes from his disciples and his critics.

$$a^2 + b^2 = c^2$$

TRANSPORTATION

The Greek mainland and islands are surrounded by water. The terrain is mountainous, and the ancient Greeks had few roads. They mainly traveled by ship. When they traveled on land, it was usually on foot. The thinker Socrates once walked from Athens to Olympia, a total of 200 miles (320 km), in five or six days.

Cargo ship

Ancient Greece relied on shipping, both to communicate with the many islands and to carry trade goods and settlers throughout the Mediterranean. Earlier vessels had curved prows and one row of oars.

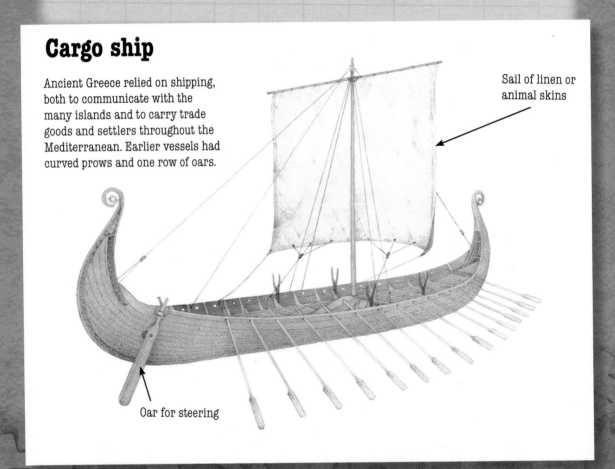

Sail of linen or animal skins

Oar for steering

Pharos at Alexandria

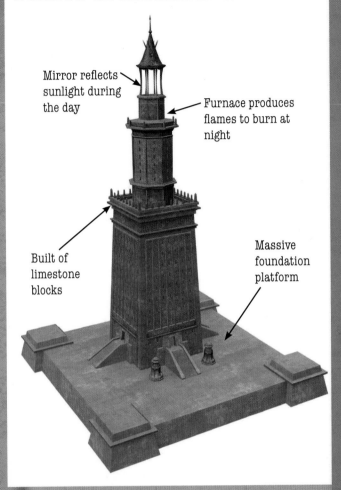

Mirror reflects sunlight during the day

Furnace produces flames to burn at night

Built of limestone blocks

Massive foundation platform

TECHNICAL SPECS

- Sea travel was dangerous because of pirates, bad weather, and poor navigation. The Greeks built the world's first lighthouse (Pharos) at Alexandria to guide ships safely into the harbor.
- The Dioklos railway was a paved road of limestone blocks. Two parallel grooves 5 feet (1.5 m) apart held the wheels of trolleys pushed by slaves.
- The ancient Greeks improved Babylonian maps. They invented both latitude and longitude and the major lines of latitude, such as the Equator, the Tropic of Cancer, and the Tropic of Capricorn.

LAND TRANSPORTATION

A cart track allowed goods to be carried the 5 miles (8 km) between the port of Piraeus and Athens. For short journeys, chariots were used; for longer distances, some people went by mule. Horses were rarely used: the Greeks had no saddles, stirrups, or horseshoes. The Greeks built a railway, Dioklos, that ran 4 miles (6.4 km) across the Isthmus of Corinth. This was a major engineering achievement. It meant small warships or empty cargo vessels could be pulled across the isthmus rather than having to sail around the peninsula.

WARSHIPS

A trireme rams an enemy vessel. Triremes had a few armed soldiers on deck ready to board a rammed ship.

Athens, the most powerful of the Greek city-states, controlled its empire by means of its navy. The Athenians called their navy their "wooden walls." By controlling the Aegean Sea, the Athenians could decide which goods and which troops went to and from the islands. The warships also protected Athens' merchant vessels from attack as they brought food and luxuries to the port of Piraeus.

The ancient Greeks had one type of warship: the trireme. This wooden galley was powered by up to 170 oarsmen sitting in three rows. At its most powerful, the city-state of Athens had 300 triremes in service.

RAMMING TACTICS

At its bow, below the waterline, the trireme had a long wooden ram covered in bronze. To sink an enemy ship, the trireme would ram it in the side. If the enemy boat did not sink, soldiers boarded it. Crews spent long periods practicing ramming and boarding maneuvers.

TECHNICAL SPECS

- The name trireme comes from the three banks of oars.
- Triremes dominated the Mediterranean between the seventh and fourth centuries B.C.E.
- A piper or drummer sometimes played a beat on the trireme to keep the rowing in time.
- Three main types of wood were used in construction: fir, pine, and cedar. Oak was used for the hulls. The ships had to be light enough to be carried ashore.
- In favorable sailing conditions, a trireme could cover up to 60 miles (96 km) in a day.

Trireme cross-section

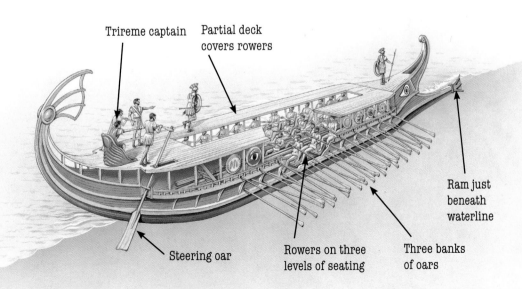

Trireme captain

Partial deck covers rowers

Steering oar

Rowers on three levels of seating

Three banks of oars

Ram just beneath waterline

WEAPONS AND WARFARE

The ancient Greek city-states often fought each other. Many Greek men joined an army. In Athens, boys trained as soldiers between the ages of 18 and 20 and could then be called up for military service. In Sparta, the organization of the whole state was based on warfare. Hoplite warriors controlled the land; the trireme controlled the seas.

Hoplites fought in close formations known as phalanxes. Their shields overlapped to form a wall.

Spartan hoplites prepare to raid enemy territory. Sparta was the most warlike of the city-states.

Between the seventh and fourth centuries B.C.E., the hoplite dominated warfare. Hoplites came from wealthy families, who paid for their armor and weapons. Poorer soldiers often served as archers and stone-slingers.

SIEGE WARFARE

Sieges were an important part of warfare. Armies used catapults, flamethrowers, and stone-slingers to defeat a walled city. The defenders dropped cauldrons of burning coals and sulfur on attackers.

TECHNICAL SPECS

- The breastplate consisted of two metal plates joined at the sides by leather straps. The sides of the upper body were left exposed.
- Helmets were vital, because when hoplites marched in a phalanx, their heads were left exposed.
- Military commanders were called strategoi, the source of the English word "strategy."
- Cavalrymen would not willingly charge a phalanx as they and the horses risked being speared.
- Phalanxes tried to break a gap in the opposing phalanx to attack the enemy's flanks and rear.
- Shields had extra strength from the loop for the hoplite's arm. There was also a handle to grip.

ASTRONOMY

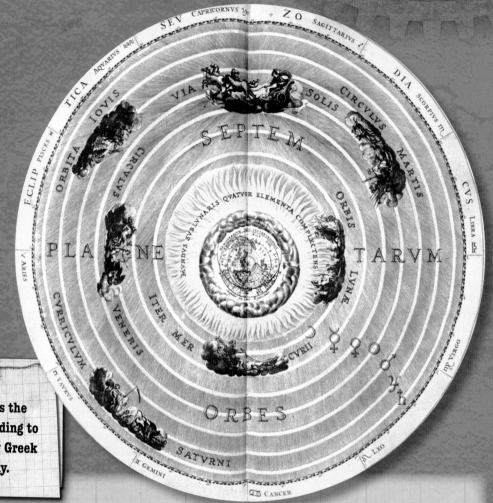

This diagram shows the solar system according to the second-century Greek astronomer Ptolemy.

The ancient Greeks contributed enormously to our understanding of astronomy, the study of heavenly bodies. They were the first people to realize Earth was round and that the moon reflected the light of the sun. They also suggested that Earth was not fixed but moved around the sun.

When the ancient Greek scientist and natural philosopher Thales of Miletus (c.624–545 B.C.E.) visited Egypt in 600 B.C.E., he returned with a knowledge of Babylonian astronomy and math. Introducing math to the study of the planets and stars was a huge breakthrough in astronomy.

UNDERSTANDING THE SKIES

Early Greeks had seen the heavenly bodies as gods that controlled their lives. Anaxagoras (c.500–428 B.C.E.) was the first person to suggest that the sun was not a god but a burning mass of metal. Once the Greeks stopped seeing heavenly bodies as gods, they started to calculate the movements of the planets and stars. This allowed them to predict the changing seasons, which was vital help for sailors and farmers.

TECHNICAL SPECS

- The Greeks understood orbits. Each month they saw the moon apparently shrink and grow, which was unlikely. They reasoned something was passing in front of it.
- Astronomers knew about the planets Mercury, Venus, Mars, Jupiter, and Saturn.
- Aristarchus of Samos (3rd century B.C.E.) suggested that Earth rotates on its axis and the sun is stationary, both of which were proved true centuries later.
- Eratosthenes of Cyrene (3rd century B.C.E.) worked out the circumference of Earth as 25,000 miles (40,225 km). The correct figure is actually 24,902 miles (40,075 km).

A medieval illustration shows the goddess of astronomy instructing Ptolemy about the heavens.

MEASURING TIME

Discovered in an ancient shipwreck, the Antikythera mechanism was made about 100 B.C.E. to calculate the movement of heavenly bodies.

The ancient Greeks needed to record the changing seasons so they knew when to plant and harvest their crops. In the ninth century B.C.E., the poet Hesiod noted that the cry of migrating cranes was the sign that it was time for farmers to plow and sow. Beyond that, each city-state followed its own calendar.

MEASURING TIME

The first water clocks were pottery jars with holes for water to drip through. A large public water clock in Athens, however, had a marker on the outside to show the time. Later clocks were more intricate. Andronichos designed the "tower of the winds" in the first century B.C.E. A complicated water clock gave the time on the sundial on top of the tower, while a rotating disk showed the movements of the stars and the course of the sun through the constellations.

TECHNICAL SPECS

- A Greek day went from sunset to sunset (not midnight to midnight as our day goes).
- Like other ancient cultures, the Greeks had 12 hours of daylight and 12 of night.
- The ancient Greeks divided their year into 12 months with a 13th month added to balance the cycle every eight years from the 5th to the middle of the 4th century B.C.E.
- Different states started their years at different times. The Athenians kept three calendars. One was for religious festivals. The second was political. The third was astronomical.
- A water clock invented by Ctesibius of Alexandria in 270 B.C.E. used valves to drive ringing bells, moving puppets, and singing birds.

Advanced water clock

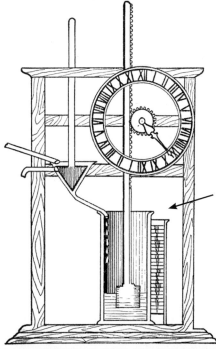

Water supply drips into tank, raising float

In this water clock, a float rising in the main tank of water raises a toothed rod, which turns a toothed cog to rotate the hand on a clock face, indicating the passage of time.

METALS AND COINS

The early ancient Greeks bartered for goods, but by 600 B.C.E., trade was flourishing and payment in coins became common. The first coins were lumps of precious metal. Precious metals were common. The silver mine at Laurium made Athens wealthy.

The tunnels in Greek mines could be as deep as 330 feet (100 m) and working conditions were extremely harsh. Slaves worked in the mines, using picks and iron hammers to extract the ore.

This silver coin was minted in Athens in the fifth century B.C.E. It features an owl, the symbol of Athena, goddess of wisdom.

- Coinage was introduced into Greece from Lydia in Asia Minor (modern-day Turkey).
- In ancient Athens, a skilled worker earned one silver drachma per day; one-sixth of a drachma was an obol.
- Pure gold coins were only used after the fourth century B.C.E. Less valuable bronze coins appeared at the end of the fifth century B.C.E.
- Since coinage was a mark of independence, every city had its own mint.
- Greek mines included not just the silver mine at Laurium, but also iron, gold, and copper mines.

Bronze was used for weapons and armor. In the fifth century B.C.E., the Athenians tipped their swords with even harder steel.

The first coins in Greece were made from electrum, an alloy of gold and silver. From the sixth century B.C.E., the usual metal for coins was pure silver. Each city-state had its own coinage. Athenian silver coins were stamped with an owl. It was the symbol of wisdom and of Athena, the goddess of the city.

EARLY COINAGE

As the number of coins in circulation increased, industries developed that were based on money. Money exchange and banking became common professions in the late fifth century B.C.E.

MEDICINE

The ancient Greeks took a huge step forward in medicine. Although they believed that sickness could be caused by the gods, they realized that good health was also a result of a person's behavior, environment, and diet. To reflect this, ancient Greek medicine combined two types of treatment. One was based on magic and the other on examining the patient and keeping him or her healthy.

The Greek god of medicine and healing was Asclepius, a son of the god Apollo. Healing took place in his temples. Greeks went to sleep there when they were sick or left gifts for the gods.

The ruins of the Asclepion still stand at Epidaurus. Snakes were considered sacred, so were allowed to crawl around the temple.

A doctor examines a patient with an injured arm. Doctors could set broken limbs but tried to avoid surgery.

The Greeks believed Asclepius appeared in a "magical dream," in which he prescribed treatments such as herbal remedies, diets, and exercise. The following day, priests at the temple would administer these cures.

HIPPOCRATES

The cult of Asclepius led to the development of medical treatments for all kinds of diseases. The greatest advances came in the Hellenistic period (323–30 B.C.E.). But the most influential doctor was Hippocrates (c.460–c.370 B.C.E.). He was the first to describe many diseases such as the clubbing of fingers (when fingers go purple, which is a sign of lung disease).

TECHNICAL SPECS

- In 400 B.C.E., Hippocrates wrote down rules about how a physician should treat a patient. Physicians still swear the Hippocratic Oath before they can practice medicine.
- Physicians tried to avoid surgery, because they saw that patients became sick after surgery from shock, loss of blood, or infections.
- The Greeks were the first people to make sure that all their cities had public fountains to supply clean water to maintain health.
- The first medical school opened at Cnidus around 700 B.C.E. Physicians there learned to observe their patients' symptoms.
- Alcmaeon, who wrote the first study of human anatomy between about 500 and 450 B.C.E., worked at the medical school at Cnidus.

POTTERY

Ancient Greek pottery is one of the best sources of information about daily life two thousand years ago. The Greeks decorated pottery with all kinds of scenes, and while few paintings and little writing have survived, many pots and pottery fragments have.

An Athenian potter shapes a vase on a wheel. Pottery was normally made and painted by different people, like a modern-day production line.

The earliest ancient Greek pots were decorated with geometric patterns. In the seventh century B.C.E., potters in Corinth began making pots with black figures cut into the clay.

POTTERY PEAK

The peak of ancient Greek pottery was the Athenian period from the sixth to fourth centuries B.C.E. In the black-figure technique, they painted figures on pots in special slip (wet clay) that turned black during firing. Around 530 B.C.E., the red-figure technique was introduced. Now the pot was black, but areas that were not painted with slip showed through as red figures.

It was easier to show detail in red-figure technique, because black-figure technique only allowed the creation of silhouettes.

TECHNICAL SPECS

- Larger pots were made in stages using a potter's wheel. The neck and body were thrown separately and joined together. The feet and handles were attached later.
- Ancient Greek pots were fired in three stages. In the first stage, air was let into the kiln. This turned the whole vase the color of the red clay. In the next stage, green wood was burned to reduce the oxygen supply. The pot turned black in the smoke. In the final stage, air was reintroduced to the kiln; unpainted areas turned back to red, while the painted areas remained black.
  - There were specific vessels for carrying food and wine (amphora), drawing water (hydria), and for drinking water and wine (kantharos or kylix).
  - The metallic glaze of the black slip was created by using illitic clay, which had low calcium oxide and was collected from local clay beds.

GLASSMAKING

These glass vessels were made near the end of the ancient Greek period, in about the fifth century C.E.

Like the ancient Egyptians and Romans, the ancient Greeks prized glassware. They did not know about glassblowing until late in their history. Instead, the Greeks produced their glassware using first the core method and then a method known as slumping. As glassmakers became more skilled, the size of the objects they produced grew larger.

The Mesopotamians first made glass around 3500 B.C.E. from a mixture of quartz sand (silica), soda, and lime. Like them, the early Greeks made glassware using the core method. The hot glass mixture was poured over a core made from clay. Once the glass had cooled, the core was scraped out.

COLORED GLASS

Later, the Greeks poured viscous glass into molds to make shapes. To make multicolored glass, threads of glass colored by adding oxides were shaped around the mold. This method was used to make dishes and beads, and for containers such as amphorae. Handles and feet were added later. As well as colored glass, ancient Greeks prized colorless glass. It was difficult to make as it needed to be made of pure silica and this required much higher temperatures to melt it properly.

TECHNICAL SPECS

- Glass was almost as precious as gold in ancient Greece.
- There were three terms for glass: "kyanos" referred to dark blue; shiny material, "lithos chyte" meant molten stone; and "hyalos" was everyday glass.
- Glass was present in ancient Mycenae, but no workshops have so far been discovered.
- Historians think that there was a substantial workshop on the island of Rhodes.
- Glass to be used for mosaics was cast in a flat, open mold and then cut into pieces.
- During the Hellenistic period, thin layers of gold were put between layers of transparent glass. Craftsmen also made cameo, a kind of light-colored glass on a dark glass background.

This fourth-century-C.E. glass vial has two handles so it can be lifted to the mouth for drinking.

TIMELINE

B.C.E.

c.1100 The Dark Ages begin in Greece as the Mycenaean civilization declines and the Dorians and Ionians invade.

c.800 The Greeks develop vowels to use with consonants taken from the Phoenician alphabet.

776 The first Olympic Games are held.

c.700 Gold coins are used as money in Lydia in western Anatolia (Turkey).

c.700 Glaucus of Chios is said to learn how to solder iron together.

c.650 The trireme replaces the bireme as the standard Greek warship.

c.600 Thales of Miletus introduces Babylonian math to Greece.

c.600 Sundials are used to measure time.

c.600 Theodorus of Samos is said to invent smelting ores and casting metals.

c.600 Alcmaeon writes the first book on human anatomy.

c.585 Thales of Miletus predicts a solar eclipse.

c.530 Among other discoveries, Pythagoras proposes that musical intervals are based on math and that sound is a vibration in the air.

c.479 Athens begins a golden age that lasts until 431 B.C.E.

c.450 Anaxagoras of Athens explains eclipses by proposing that the moon reflects sunlight and has no illumination of its own.

c.440 The lost wax process is used for casting objects in bronze.

c.440 Hippocrates argues that diseases have natural rather than supernatural causes.

c.425	The Thebans are said to use a flamethrower in an attack on Delium.
399	Engineers at Syracuse invent an arrow-firing catapult to defend the city.
387	Plato founds his Academy in Athens.
c.375	Archytas of Tarentum builds the first automaton (robot) and studies mechanics.
c.340	Praxagoras of Crete discovers the difference between veins and arteries.
c.335	Aristotle founds the Lyceum in Athens.
c.330	Aristotle uses the camera obscura to study projection.
327	Alexander the Great of Macedon begins his campaigns of conquest.
c.300	Euclid writes *Elements*, for centuries a standard work on geometry.
c.280	The Pharos of Alexandria is built; it is the world's first lighthouse.
c.270	Ctesibius of Alexandria invents a water clock that uses mechanical gears.
c.245	The library of Alexandria is cataloged for the first time.
c.240	Eratosthenes of Cyrene calculates the diameter of Earth.
c.225	Archimedes invents the Archimedes screw.
c.170	Parchment is invented in Pergamon; it replaces papyrus as writing material.
c.134	Hipparchus measures the year more accurately than anyone before him.

C.E.

45	Sosigenes of Alexandria devises a calendar of 365.25 days, adopted by the Roman emperor Julius Caesar (the Julian calendar).
60	Heron of Alexandria builds the first steam engine and describes many automata.

GLOSSARY

acoustics The science of sound.

acropolis Greek for "high city;" a fortified part of a city on a height. The most famous acropolis was at Athens.

city-state A city that governs itself and the surrounding territory.

crop rotation Varying the crops grown in fields to give the soil a chance to recover.

displacement The action by which an object put into water moves away an equal volume of water.

eclipse When one heavenly body passes in front of another.

frieze In architecture, a band of carved decoration, often around the top of a building.

Hellenistic Related to classical Greece.

helmsman The person in charge of steering a ship.

hoplite A Greek infantry soldier.

irrigation Artificially watering the land to grow crops.

mosaic A decoration made by using small pieces of colored glass or ceramic to cover a surface.

orchestra A circular space for performances in a Greek theater.

ore Rocks and minerals in which metals naturally occur.

phalanx A formation in which soldiers formed lines of defense with overlapping shields.

philosophy An attempt to understand reality by observation, logical thought, and deduction.

slip A mixture of clay and water used for decorating pots.

staple A food that makes up the major part of a diet.

theorem A mathematical proposal that can be shown to be true.

trireme A rowed warship with three banks of oars.

FURTHER INFORMATION

BOOKS

Apel, Melanie Ann. *Technology of Ancient Greece* (Primary Sources of Ancient Civilizations). Rosen Publishing Group, 2004.

Bordessa, Michael. *Tools of the Ancient Greeks: A Kid's Guide to the History & Science of Life in Ancient Greece*. Nomad Press, 2006.

Gow, Mary. *The Great Thinker: Aristotle and the Foundations of Science* (Great Minds of Ancient Science and Math). Enslow Publishing Inc., 2010.

Maynard, Charles W. *The Technology of Ancient Greece* (The Technology of the Ancient World). Rosen Publishing Group, 2006.

Platt, Richard, and David Lawrence. *The Greeks* (How They Made Things Work!). Sea to Sea Publications, 2011.

Snedden, Robert. *Ancient Greece* (Technology in Times Past). Smart Apple Media, 2008.

WEBSITES

www.britishmuseum.org/explore/cultures/europe/ancient Greece.aspx
British Museum guide to ancient Greece.

www.primaryresources.co.uk/history/history5b.htm
Primarysources.com page with links to ancient Greek subjects.

www.swan.ac.uk/grst/
Pages hosted by Swansea University about technology in ancient Greece and Rome.

Publisher's note to educators and parents: Our editors have carefully reviewed these websites to ensure that they are suitable for students. Many websites change frequently, however, and we cannot guarantee that a site's future contents will continue to meet our high standards of quality and educational value. Be advised that students should be closely supervised whenever they access the Internet.

INDEX